Exploring the Bible

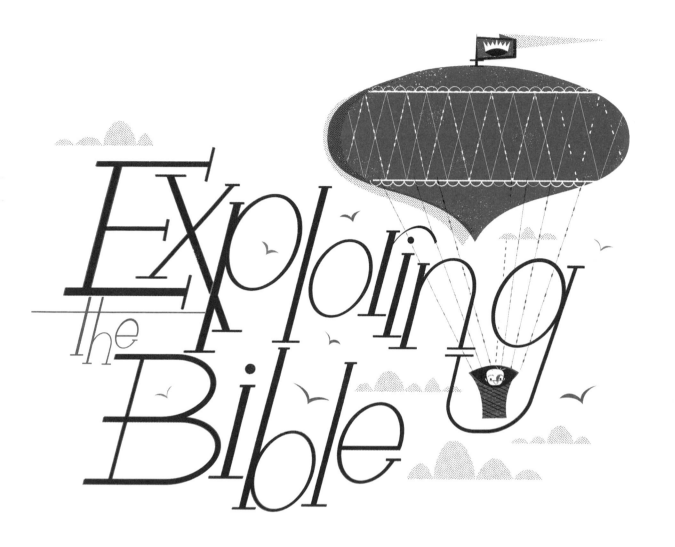

Exploring the Bible

A Bible Reading Plan for Kids

David Murray

Artwork by Scotty Reifsnyder

 **CROSSWAY**®

WHEATON, ILLINOIS

Trade paperback ISBN: 978-1-4335-5686-9
PDF ISBN: 978-1-4335-5687-6

Library of Congress Cataloging-in-Publication Data

Names: Murray, David, 1966 May 28- author. | Reifsnyder, Scotty, illustrator.
Title: Exploring the Bible : a bible reading plan for kids / David Murray ; artwork by Scott Reifsnyder.
Description: Wheaton, Illinois : Crossway, 2017. | Audience: Ages 6-12.
Identifiers: LCCN 2017008202 (print) | ISBN 9781433556876 (pdf) | ISBN 9781433556869 (tp)
Subjects: LCSH: Bible—Introductions—Juvenile literature. | Bible—Reading—Juvenile literature.
Classification: LCC BS539 .M87 2014 (print) | DDC 220.6/1—dc23
LC record available at https://lccn.loc.gov/2017008202

Crossway is a publishing ministry of Good News Publishers.

RRD		27	26	25	24	23	22	21	20	19	18	17
15	14	13	12	11	10	9	8	7	6	5	4	3	2	1

FOREWORD

I didn't know it at the time, but one of the greatest blessings in my life was being trained at a very early age to read the Bible every day. My dad modeled daily Bible reading and lovingly encouraged me in the practice. My mother made sure I had adequate lighting above my bed, the place where I did most of my childhood reading. We attended a church where my Sunday school teachers asked every week if each of us boys had read the Bible every day. But this was more than a mere expectation, because the quarterly literature they gave us for the class contained a daily Bible reading plan to guide our intake of Scripture for the next three months. Legalistic? Well, any sort of structure in the Christian life can contribute to legalism *if* one is inclined that way. But I was a child, and we all—especially children—need some structure when beginning to learn something as big and important as the Bible.

Without guidance and a plan, children will flounder when trying to read and understand the Bible on their own. That's why resources like this book are so important. I don't even want to imagine what my Christian life and my ministry would have been without the encouragement and structure for daily Bible reading I received as a child. But if I'd had something like *Exploring the Bible*, I think my scriptural foundations would have been even stronger. Blessed beyond their knowing is the boy or girl who receives this book and the loving help to complete it.

Donald S. Whitney, professor of biblical spirituality, associate dean,
School of Theology, The Southern Baptist Theological Seminary, Louisville, KY

EXPLORING THE BIBLE

We were totally lost with no idea which way to turn. A few hours earlier forty of us boys and six adult leaders had set out to climb a mountain near our church's summer camp.

We started out with great excitement as we looked forward to the challenges on the way to the summit: a mysterious forest, swampy fields, fast-flowing streams, sharp rocks, slippery paths, and steep climbs. But it would all be worth it for the view at the top.

But now we were wet, tired, hungry, cold, scared, and very, very lost.

LOST ON A MOUNTAIN

What went wrong?

Our leaders had forgotten to check the weather forecast, which would have warned them about the fog and rain that met us halfway up the mountain. They had also failed to provide us with maps, compasses, and whistles, in case we got separated from the main group.

And now, four of my friends and I were on the side of a cold and dangerous mountain, with no leader, no compass, no map, no food, no raincoats, and no idea where to go. We longed for someone to appear out of the mist to show us where to go next and lead us home. We'd long given up hope of reaching the summit. Obviously, I'm here to tell the tale, so I must have survived! If you hang around, I'll tell you how.

LOST IN THE BIBLE?

Perhaps sometimes you feel lost and confused when reading the Bible. You start to read it as an excited explorer, looking forward to discovering amazing truths about God and the gospel. But after a few chapters you feel lost in a fog, not knowing where you are or where to go. You keep trying to push forward but you lack a leader, a map, and a compass. You wish someone would not only help you take the next step but also lead you to the summit so that you might see the Christian faith in a new and wonderful way.

That's where this book, *Exploring the Bible*, comes to your rescue. It will act as your leader, map, and compass to the Bible. It won't take you to every part of the Bible, but it will take you to the main peaks and give you an all-round view of its beautiful landscape. At times we'll slow down and look at some parts more closely. Other times, we'll speed up in order to get to the next major mountain peak in the Bible's story. By the end of a year, you'll have learned skills to help you explore the Bible on your own with safety and success.

EXPEDITION

We'll go on one expedition a week. Unlike my disastrous camp, we'll begin each expedition with a plan to map out the chapters of the Bible we're about to explore.

PRAYER POINTS

We'll then pray for God's blessing on our travels and write down a couple of extra prayer points for the week. For example, we might pray for help with schoolwork. Or we could pray for our parents, our friends, our church, or for different nations and the missionaries that work there.

SNAPSHOT

I still have a couple of photos from my doomed climbing trip. Every time I look at us, soaked by the rain and surrounded by fog, the bad memories come flooding back.

But I want us to take snapshots of our expeditions that will bring back good memories. That's why I've selected a memory verse from each week's trip. Write it out from your Bible, and then try to memorize a bit of it each day so that you will build up a bank of wonderful memories from your travels.

DAILY LOG

The daily log has a title that sums up that day's trip and a note of what verses to read. It has space to write out a verse or answer a question. That's to help us keep thinking about what we have been reading and to remind us of what we have learned along the way.

EXPLORING WITH OTHERS

Sunday is rest-and-recharge day. Instead of continuing our march through the Bible, we'll pause and think about what we've learned from the past week. We'll look ahead to what God will show us later in the Bible. And we'll think about how to live out the Christian life. This is where it's good to involve Dad or Mom. Perhaps ask them to look at your daily log and chat with them about anything you found difficult.

They can also help you with the discussion questions, which are designed to connect our week's reading with the rest of the Bible and with our lives.

Another fellow-explorer we can learn from is our pastor. He's an experienced traveler in the Bible and can teach us how to explore it better. That's why there's space in the log for you to write down your pastor's sermon text and his main sermon points, and what you will do in response to his message.

I'm looking forward to exploring the Bible with you and enjoying the beautiful views of God and of salvation that we will discover.

Oh, yes, I almost forgot to tell you how my friends and I were rescued. A strong wind blew away the fog so that we saw a road in a distant valley. When we got to the road, we flagged down a driver who then took us all the way back to our camp. I hope this book will blow away the fog from the Bible and lead you along a road that takes you all the way home to Jesus Christ.

Your Fellow Explorer,
David Murray

EXPLORING WITH OTHERS

SUNDAY | Enjoying the View

That was a horrible journey, wasn't it? We might even be tempted to try and forget about what we saw. Yet it does help us understand what's gone wrong with us and our world. And we also saw that bright spot where God provides great hope of salvation from sin and evil. Look ahead with hope to Romans 16:20. Who is the Devil-crusher?

Sermon Title

Sermon Text

Sermon Notes

My Response

EXPEDITION 3: A FLOODED WORLD

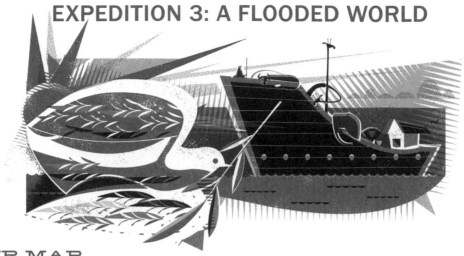

OUR MAP

Hundreds of years have passed since our last expedition. As we look around, we will see lots of people and lots of sin. That's what God saw, and that's why he destroyed the world with a flood. But we won't just see a dreadful deluge this week; we'll once again see God's beautiful mercy in saving Noah, his family, and many animals in an ark.

PRAYER POINTS

SNAPSHOT VERSE

Genesis 6:8

DAILY LOG

MONDAY | God Hates Sin

 Genesis 6:1–4

 What did God say about his Holy Spirit (v. 3)?

TUESDAY | God Gives Grace to Noah

 Genesis 6:5–8

 What did God see (v. 5)?

WEDNESDAY | God Warns Noah

 Genesis 6:9–14

 How does Genesis describe Noah (v. 9)?

THURSDAY | God Covenants with Noah

 Genesis 6:17–22

 What did God establish with Noah (v. 18)? (A *covenant* is a special promise from God.)

FRIDAY | God Remembers Noah

 Genesis 8:1–5

 Where did the ark come to rest (v. 4)?

SATURDAY | God Gives Promises to Noah

 Genesis 9:12–17

 Genesis 9:13

EXPLORING WITH OTHERS

SUNDAY | Enjoying the View

If we pause and look down the road of history, we can see how God later used Noah's flood to teach us big lessons. What does the Noah story tell us about end of the world and how to be ready for it (Matthew 24:37–39)?

Sermon Title

Sermon Text

Sermon Notes

My Response

EXPEDITION 4: A SPECIAL PROMISE OF A SPECIAL SON

OUR MAP

As the world population grew again after the flood, so did its sin. The desperate situation came to a climax with the Tower of Babel in Genesis 11. God judged the proud builders of this tower by confusing their language and scattering them. Against this dark background, once again God showed how loving he is. He picked out one man, Abram, and promised him a special son who would bring blessing to the whole world.

PRAYER POINTS

SNAPSHOT VERSE

Genesis 15:6

DAILY LOG

MONDAY | God Promises Abram a Great Blessing

 Genesis 12:1–5

 What will God do to (a) Abram's friends and (b) Abram's enemies (v. 3)?

TUESDAY | God Promises Abram a Son

 Genesis 15:1–6

 What did God say to Abram (v. 1)?

WEDNESDAY | God Tests Abram's Patience

 Genesis 16:1–6

 What did Abram do when Sarai had no children (v. 3)?

THURSDAY | God Covenants with Abram

 Genesis 17:1–5

 What does Abram's new name mean (v. 5)?

FRIDAY | God Commands Abraham to Be Circumcised

 Genesis 17:6–10

 Genesis 17:7

SATURDAY | God Assures Abraham

 Genesis 17:15–22

 Why was it so difficult for Abraham to believe that he would have a child (v. 17)?

EXPLORING WITH OTHERS

SUNDAY | Enjoying the View

Look way ahead into the New Testament and see how God uses the story of Abraham. What does God want us to learn about salvation from Abraham's story (Genesis 15:6; Romans 4:1–5)?

Sermon Title

Sermon Text

Sermon Notes

My Response

EXPEDITION 5: A LONG AND PAINFUL TEST

OUR MAP

We're going to follow Abraham and watch how God tests his faith by making him wait and wait for the promised son. Despite many ups and downs in Abraham's faith, and despite a mix of successes and failures, God at last blesses him with a boy named Isaac.

PRAYER POINTS

SNAPSHOT VERSE

Genesis 22:14

DAILY LOG

MONDAY | Abraham's Son Is Born

 Genesis 21:1–7

 What promise did God keep (vv. 1–2)?

TUESDAY | Another Son Is Protected

 Genesis 21:8–13

 Why was Ishmael put out of the home (v. 9)?

WEDNESDAY | Abraham's Son Is to Die

 Genesis 22:1–5

 What did God command Abraham to do to Isaac (v. 2)?

THURSDAY | Abraham Lays His Son on the Altar of Sacrifice

 Genesis 22:6–10

 What did Abraham say to Isaac (v. 8)?

FRIDAY | Abraham Finds a Substitute for His Son

 Genesis 22:11–14

 What did Abraham do with the ram (v. 13)?

SATURDAY | Abraham's Son Will Be a Great Blessing

 Genesis 22:15–19

 How will God bless the nations (v. 18)?

EXPLORING WITH OTHERS

SUNDAY | Enjoying the View

We've been following Abraham's footsteps closely this week. Let's pause, step out of his shadow, and ask ourselves two big questions: Who are the children of Abraham (Galatians 3:6–7)? Are you a child of Abraham?

Sermon Title

Sermon Text

Sermon Notes

My Response

EXPEDITION 6: SAVED FROM SLAVERY

OUR MAP

This expedition starts a few hundred years after our last one. God's promise to increase Abraham's family was fulfilled through his son Isaac, and then through Isaac's son Jacob. Because of a famine, Jacob and his sons ended up in Egypt, where God had sent Joseph (another of Jacob's sons) many years earlier so that he would one day be able to save his family from starvation (Genesis 37–50). God continued to multiply this special family despite the Egyptians' treating them badly (Exodus 1–2). Let's pause and take a closer look at how God raised up a deliverer, Moses, to save Israel from Egyptian slavery.

 PRAYER POINTS

 **SNAPSHOT VERSE** | Exodus 14:13

DAILY LOG

MONDAY | God Calls His Savior

 Exodus 2:23–3:6

 What did God remember when he heard Israel's groaning (2:24)?

TUESDAY | God Sends His Savior

 Exodus 3:7–10

 What did God send Moses to do (v. 10)?

WEDNESDAY | God Reveals Himself to His Savior

 Exodus 3:11–15

 What was Moses to say to the Israelites (v. 15)?

Bridge: We're going to skip a few chapters that describe how Pharaoh, the king of Egypt, refused to release the Israelites. God sent lots of plagues on the Egyptians, including frogs and insects, to persuade Pharaoh to let God's people go (Exodus 7–11). We pick up the story with the last and most serious plague, the death of all the firstborn in Egypt.

THURSDAY | God Provides a Substitute Lamb

 Exodus 12:1–7, 24–28

 Describe the lamb that was to be sacrificed (v. 5).

Bridge: Pharaoh eventually agreed to let the Israelites go, but after they left, he had a change of heart and tried to get them back. Let's see what happened next.

FRIDAY | God Saves from Slavery, the Sea, and the Soldiers

 Exodus 14:10–14, 30–31

 What were the Israelites to do (v. 13)?

SATURDAY | God's Salvation Is Praised

 Exodus 15:1–6

 How does Moses describe God (v. 2)?

EXPLORING WITH OTHERS

SUNDAY | Enjoying the View

God used Moses to save Israel in the Old Testament. Who is God's Savior in the New Testament (Matthew 20:28; Hebrews 3:1–3)? God used the lamb to save Israel in the Old Testament. Who is God's Lamb in the New Testament (1 Corinthians 5:7; 1 Peter 1:19)?

Sermon Title

Sermon Text

Sermon Notes

My Response

EXPEDITION 7: A NEW NATION

OUR MAP

God saved Israel from Egypt, made them a new nation, and then gave them important laws. These laws helped them to live and worship in a way that pleased God.

PRAYER POINTS

SNAPSHOT VERSE

Exodus 20:2

DAILY LOG

MONDAY | Obedience Follows Salvation

 Exodus 19:1-6

 Why should Israel obey God (v. 4)?

TUESDAY | Obedience for the Glory of God

 Exodus 20:1-7

 Exodus 20:3

WEDNESDAY | Obedience for the Benefit of Others

 Exodus 20:8-17

 Exodus 20:12

THURSDAY | God's Glorious House

 Exodus 25:1–8

 Why did God want Israel to build him a house (v. 8)?

FRIDAY | God's Glorious Name

 Exodus 34:5–9

 How does God describe himself (v. 6)?

SATURDAY | God's Glorious Presence

 Exodus 40:34–38

 What filled the tabernacle (v. 34)?

EXPLORING WITH OTHERS

SUNDAY | Enjoying the View

We've just seen God's presence come down to earth and fill the tabernacle. Now look ahead to see another time when God's presence came down to earth in a glorious way (John 1:14). What is more glorious—God filling a house or God filling a human?

Sermon Title

Sermon Text

Sermon Notes

My Response

EXPEDITION 8: BLOOD AND DUST

OUR MAP

This week we will travel to two unusual places. The first is the book of Leviticus, which is full of animal blood and teaches us how God forgives sin. The second is the book of Numbers, which is full of desert dust and teaches us how God punishes sin.

PRAYER POINTS

SNAPSHOT VERSE

Hebrews 10:12 (It's in the New Testament.)

DAILY LOG

MONDAY | A Blood Sacrifice

 Leviticus 1:1–5

 Where was the animal to be killed (v. 5)?

TUESDAY | A Burned Sacrifice

 Leviticus 1:6–9

 Where was the sacrifice to be placed (v. 8)?

WEDNESDAY | A Sweet-Smelling Sacrifice

 Leviticus 1:10–13

 What did the Lord think of the sacrifice (last words of vv. 9 and 13)?

THURSDAY | Complaints in the Desert

 Numbers 14:1–5

 What did the Israelites want to do (v. 4)?

FRIDAY | Death in the Desert

 Numbers 14:26–32

 Why was God angry with Israel (v. 27)?

SATURDAY | Salvation in the Desert

 Numbers 21:4–9

 Numbers 21:8

EXPLORING WITH OTHERS

SUNDAY | Enjoying the View

What did the Old Testament sacrifices preview (John 1:29)?
Many years later, what did Jesus say must be lifted up in the wilderness (John 3:14–15)?

Sermon Title

Sermon Text

Sermon Notes

My Response

EXPEDITION 9: LOOK BACK, LOOK FORWARD, LOOK UP

OUR MAP

In the book of Deuteronomy, we look backward, forward, and upward. We look backward at all that God did for Israel. He delivered them from Egypt, gave them his laws, and led them through the desert for forty years. Then we look forward to the land of Canaan, which God had promised to give to Israel. Finally, we look upward as we follow Moses up a mountain and enjoy his spectacular view of Canaan just before God takes him to heaven. The book finishes with Israel's new leader, Joshua.

PRAYER POINTS

SNAPSHOT VERSE

Deuteronomy 33:27a (Finish the verse at "arms.")

DAILY LOG

MONDAY | Moses Looks Back to the Desert

 Deuteronomy 8:1–6

 What were the Israelites to remember (v. 2)?

TUESDAY | Moses Looks Ahead to the Promised Land

 Deuteronomy 8:7–11

 What were the Israelites to do when they had eaten well (v. 10)?

WEDNESDAY | Moses Looks Up to God

 Deuteronomy 8:12–18

 Why were the Israelites to remember God (v. 18)?

THURSDAY | Moses Looks at Israel's Happiness

 Deuteronomy 33:26–29

 Why was Israel so happy (v. 29)?

FRIDAY | Moses Goes to Heaven

 Deuteronomy 34:1–6

 What promise was God keeping (v. 4)?

SATURDAY | Moses Replaced by Joshua

 Deuteronomy 34:7–12

 Describe Joshua, Israel's next leader (v. 9).

EXPLORING WITH OTHERS

SUNDAY | Enjoying the View

In Deuteronomy 18:15–19 God promises that he will raise up a prophet who will be like Moses. Who is the prophet who is like Moses but also better than Moses (Acts 3:22–26)?

Sermon Title

Sermon Text

Sermon Notes

My Response

EXPEDITION 10: ENTERING THE PROMISED LAND

OUR MAP

Under Joshua's leadership, Israel marched into the Promised Land of Canaan and began to live in it. Everything looked great for the Israelites. However, they soon began to reject God's leaders and God's laws. In the book of Judges, we see what happens to people when they reject God and just do whatever they want.

 PRAYER POINTS

 SNAPSHOT VERSE | Judges 21:25

DAILY LOG

MONDAY | God Provides a New Leader for Israel

 Joshua 1:1-5

 What did God promise Joshua (v. 5)?

TUESDAY | God Promises Israel His Presence

 Joshua 1:6-9

 What did God command Joshua (v. 9)?

WEDNESDAY | Israel Cries to God

 Judges 2:1-5

 What did the Israelites do when God showed them their sin (v. 4)?

THURSDAY | Israel Forgets God

 Judges 2:6–10

 Describe the people after Joshua died (v. 10).

FRIDAY | Israel Follows Other Gods

 Judges 2:11–15

 What was Israel's sin against God (v. 12)?

SATURDAY | God Pities Israel

 Judges 2:16–19

 What happened when the judges died (v. 19)?

EXPLORING WITH OTHERS

SUNDAY | Enjoying the View

That was a disappointing expedition, wasn't it? It started off so brightly under Joshua's leadership, but by the time of the judges, the darkness is falling. At the end of Judges, we are told four times that Israel had no king, and therefore the people did just what they wanted. But let's end our trip on a bright note by looking forward to a new and better King who will deliver God's people and bless them with obedience. Look up Luke 1:31–33 and describe this great King.

Sermon Title

Sermon Text

Sermon Notes

My Response

EXPEDITION 11: A BAD KING AND A GOOD KING

OUR MAP

On our trip through Joshua and Judges we saw how much Israel needed a king. We don't have time to stop in the book of Ruth, but it's fascinating to see that it ends with Ruth's family tree. Whose name is last in that list? It's David (Ruth 4:18–23). That's why we set out into the books of 1 and 2 Samuel looking for a king named David. Unfortunately, Israel took a wrong turn and chose their own king, a man named Saul, who turned out badly. We pick up the story with the prophet Samuel trying to find God's choice of a king to replace the people's choice.

PRAYER POINTS

SNAPSHOT VERSE

1 Samuel 16:7b (starts with "For the LORD")

DAILY LOG

MONDAY | God Rejects the People's King

 1 Samuel 16:1–5

 Where would Samuel find God's King (v. 1)?

TUESDAY | God Chooses the King

 1 Samuel 16:6–10

 What does God look at most (v. 7)?

WEDNESDAY | Samuel Anoints God's King

 1 Samuel 16:11–14

 What did the Spirit of the Lord do (vv. 13–14)?

THURSDAY | God's King Is Brave

 1 Samuel 17:32-37

 Who is the Philistine (vv. 4, 32)?

FRIDAY | God's King Fights Evil

 1 Samuel 17:41-49

 In whose name did David come to Goliath (v. 45)?

SATURDAY | God's King Wins

 1 Samuel 17:50-54

 1 Samuel 17:50

EXPLORING WITH OTHERS

David, God's chosen king, beat Goliath, the great enemy of God's people. Can you think of another King who beat an even greater enemy (Hebrews 2:14)? What was his weapon?

Sermon Title

Sermon Text

Sermon Notes

My Response

EXPEDITION 12: A SPECIAL PROMISE OF A SPECIAL KING

OUR MAP

David was Israel's greatest king, and we'd love to spend time exploring the details of his life. However, because we need to keep moving, our explorations will have to pick the most important events. This week we're going to look at the highest point in his life—the special covenant promises God gave to him. Then we're going to look at the lowest point in David's life—when he committed terrible sins.

 ## PRAYER POINTS

 ## SNAPSHOT VERSE | 2 Samuel 7:16

DAILY LOG

MONDAY | God Makes Great Promises

 2 Samuel 7:12–17

 What does God promise David (v. 16)?

TUESDAY | David Humbly Replies

 2 Samuel 7:18–24

 What questions does David ask (v. 18)

WEDNESDAY | David Sins

 2 Samuel 11:1–5

 Which commandment did David break (Exodus 20:14)?

THURSDAY | Nathan Illustrates David's Sin

 2 Samuel 12:1–6

 In what way is David like the rich man in Nathan's story (v. 4)?

FRIDAY | Nathan Uncovers David's Sin

 2 Samuel 12:7–10

 2 Samuel 12:10

SATURDAY | David Confesses His Sin

 2 Samuel 12:11–14

 What did David say to Nathan (v. 13)?

EXPLORING WITH OTHERS

SUNDAY | Enjoying the View

More than 1,500 years after David's life, a priest named Zechariah announced that God had kept his promises to Abraham and David that a special son and a special king would save God's people from their enemies (Luke 1:68–73). Who was this special Son and special King (Luke 2:10–11)?

Sermon Title

Sermon Text

Sermon Notes

My Response

EXPEDITION 13: SONGS IN THE MIDST OF SADNESS

OUR MAP

When you sin against your mom or dad, they may have to discipline you even though they still love you. Actually, they discipline you *because* they love you. That's what we see God doing in the remaining chapters of David's life. Because God still loves him, God disciplines David with a number of sad events in his life. This includes the rebellion of his son, Absalom, which ends in Absalom's death. However, at the end of his life, we will hear David sing a beautiful song of praise to God and then some beautiful words of trust in God's promises of a greater and everlasting King.

PRAYER POINTS

SNAPSHOT VERSE

2 Samuel 22:47

DAILY LOG

MONDAY | David's Son Is Killed

 2 Samuel 18:5, 9–10, 15

 Absalom wanted to kill his father, David. Even so, what did David ask Joab to do with Absalom (v. 5)?

TUESDAY | David Weeps Over His Son

 2 Samuel 18:33–19:4

 What did David say when he heard that Absalom was dead (18:33)?

WEDNESDAY | David Sings to God His Rock

 2 Samuel 22:1–4

 What does David call God (v. 2)?

THURSDAY | David Sings to God His Shield

 2 Samuel 22:31–36

 2 Samuel 22:33

FRIDAY | David Sings to God His Salvation

 2 Samuel 22:47–51

 What does David say he will do (v. 50)?

SATURDAY | David Trusts in God's Promises

 2 Samuel 23:1–5

 2 Samuel 23:5

EXPLORING WITH OTHERS

SUNDAY | Enjoying the View

David described God as his rock when everything else in his life was like sinking sand. What foundation does the apostle Paul say we should stand upon (1 Corinthians 3:11)?

Sermon Title

Sermon Text

Sermon Notes

My Response

EXPEDITION 14: A CAPTIVE NATION

OUR MAP

Our map of the next four books of Kings and Chronicles looks messy. It's messy because the lives of Israel's kings were messy. Like King David, his son Solomon started his reign well: he built a temple for God. But he also fell into terrible sin. Just as sin separated King David's family, so sin separated King Solomon's kingdom into two parts—Israel and Judah. And as the kings and people kept on sinning, God finally separated them from the land. He sent enemies like Babylon to invade, capture the people, and take them back to Babylon as prisoners.

 PRAYER POINTS

 SNAPSHOT VERSE | 1 Kings 8:56

DAILY LOG

MONDAY | Solomon Worships God

1 Kings 8:14–21

Why did Solomon build a temple (vv. 17–20)?

TUESDAY | Solomon Worships Idols

1 Kings 11:1–6

How did Solomon compare with his father David (v. 6)?

WEDNESDAY | God Punishes Solomon

1 Kings 11:7–13

How did God punish Solomon for his sins (v. 11)?

THURSDAY | Judah's Last King

 2 Chronicles 36:11–16

 What did Israel do to God's temple (v. 14)?

FRIDAY | Judah's Punishment

 2 Chronicles 36:17–21

 Where were the people taken (v. 20)?

SATURDAY | Judah's Hope

 2 Chronicles 36:22–23

 Who made Cyrus release the people to rebuild the temple (v. 22)?

EXPLORING WITH OTHERS

SUNDAY | Enjoying the View

God had promised a godly king ruling over a godly people in a godly kingdom. Many kings, many chapters, and many miles later, we seem no closer to seeing this promise fulfilled. However, Saturday's reading should give us hope that our exploration may yet have a happy ending. Second Chronicles 36:22–23 describes what happened after God's people and God's king had been held prisoners in Babylon for seventy years. What does this tell you about God's promises? Can you think of another time of surprising hope when all seemed lost? Here's a clue: Mark 16:1–8.

Sermon Title

Sermon Text

Sermon Notes

My Response

EXPEDITION 15: A REBUILT NATION

OUR MAP

We are ready to start our expedition into the book of Ezra. God has moved the heathen King Cyrus to release God's people, allowing them to return to Jerusalem and rebuild the city and temple. Ezra and the people rebuild the temple. However, despite this progress there's still disappointment because the temple is much smaller than before, the people are still sinning, and there still is no king.

 ## PRAYER POINTS

 ## SNAPSHOT VERSE | Ezra 7:27

DAILY LOG

MONDAY | Cyrus Plans to Rebuild the Temple

 Ezra 1:1–4

 Who gave King Cyrus his power (v. 2)?

TUESDAY | The People Build the Temple

 Ezra 3:8–13

 What did the people sing when the temple-building began (v. 11)?

WEDNESDAY | The People Sin

 Ezra 9:1–4

 What did Ezra do when he heard the people had started marrying the heathen (v. 3)?

THURSDAY | Ezra Confesses the People's Sins

 Ezra 9:5–9

 Ezra 9:6

FRIDAY | Ezra Pleads for Mercy

 Ezra 9:10–15

 How had God punished the people (v. 13)?

SATURDAY | The People Confess Their Sins

 Ezra 10:1–4

 How did the people respond to God's commandment (v. 3)?

EXPLORING WITH OTHERS

SUNDAY | Enjoying the View

This story warned us about the danger of marrying those who are not believers. What does the New Testament say about this (1 Corinthians 7:39; 2 Corinthians 6:14)?

Sermon Title

Sermon Text

Sermon Notes

My Response

EXPEDITION 16: THE DEVIL ATTACKS

OUR MAP

We've now traveled over three thousand years since we started our expedition in Genesis! We've covered a lot of miles and discovered many evidences of God's love to sinners. Despite Adam's sin, God promised a King who would destroy sin and save his people. And despite the Israelites' constant sinning, God's promise still stands. We're going to pause now and travel backward a bit to look at how various poets and prophets wrote about their hope for deliverance by God's King. We'll start with Job, a man whom the Devil attacked so badly that he lost his home, his family, his wealth, and his health. But did he give up hope in God? Let's see.

 PRAYER POINTS

 SNAPSHOT VERSE | Job 19:25

DAILY LOG

MONDAY | A Godly Man

 Job 1:1–5

 Describe Job's character (v. 1).

TUESDAY | A Targeted Man

 Job 1:6–12

 What did Satan say Job would do (v. 11)?

WEDNESDAY | A Suffering Man

 Job 1:13–19

 Who was killed by the great wind (vv. 18–19)?

THURSDAY | A Worshiping Man

 Job 1:20–22

 Job 1:21

FRIDAY | A Hope-Filled Man

 Job 19:23–27

 Whom did Job expect to see (v. 26)?

Bridge: In chapters 4–37, Job's friends gave him a lot of bad counsel. Job sometimes reacted badly to this advice. However, when God gives his perfect counsel in chapters 38–41, Job was humbled.

SATURDAY | A Restored Man

 Job 42:10–16

 What did God give Job when his sufferings ended (v. 10)?

EXPLORING WITH OTHERS

SUNDAY | Enjoying the View

What hope does Job talk about in Job 19:25–27? See John 11:25 and 1 Corinthians 15:20–22.

Sermon Title

Sermon Text

Sermon Notes

My Response

EXPEDITION 17: SONGS ABOUT THE COMING KING

OUR MAP

Get your headphones on because for the next two weeks we're going to be listening to the songs God gave to his people to sing while they waited for the coming King. These songs have an unusual combination: the King is opposed, the King suffers, and the King is victorious. As you listen to these songs, think about who matches this description: an opposed King, a suffering King, and a victorious King.

 PRAYER POINTS

 SNAPSHOT VERSE | Psalm 2:12

DAILY LOG

MONDAY | The King Is Opposed

 Psalm 2:1–6

 Who opposes God's King (v. 2)?

TUESDAY | The King Is Victorious

 Psalm 2:7–12

 What will the King do to his enemies (v. 9)?

WEDNESDAY | The King Is Forsaken by God

 Psalm 22:1–5

 What is the first question the King asks God in this psalm (v. 1)?

THURSDAY | The King Is Mocked by People

 Psalm 22:6–13

 How do people react to the suffering King (v. 7)?

FRIDAY | The King Is Attacked by Beasts

 Psalm 22:14–21

 What do the people do with the King's clothes (v. 18)?

SATURDAY | The King Is Victorious

 Psalm 22:27–31

 Psalm 22:28

EXPLORING WITH OTHERS

SUNDAY | Enjoying the View

Did God ever give his people such a King? A King who was opposed, a King who suffered, and a King who finally triumphed? Here are a few clues. Read Matthew 27:35, Mark 15:34, and Acts 2:23–26 to see who matches the songs we've been listening to this week.

Sermon Title

Sermon Text

Sermon Notes

My Response

EXPEDITION 18: SONGS ABOUT THE COMING KINGDOM

OUR MAP

Now that we know who this suffering King is, let's put a spring in our step as we listen to two more beautiful songs that praise him for his glorious and everlasting kingdom.

 ## PRAYER POINTS

 **SNAPSHOT VERSE** | Psalm 72:17

DAILY LOG

MONDAY | A Just King

 Psalm 72:1–4

 How will the King rule (v. 2)?

TUESDAY | A Prosperous King

 Psalm 72:5–7

 How long will the King's kingdom last (v. 5)?

WEDNESDAY | A King of Kings

 Psalm 72:8–11

 How far will the King's kingdom extend (v. 8)?

THURSDAY | A Merciful King

 Psalm 72:12–15

 What will this King do for the poor and needy (vv. 12–13)?

FRIDAY | A Blessed King

 Psalm 72:16–20

 What will the nations call this King (v. 17)?

SATURDAY | A Praised King

 Psalm 150

 Who and what should praise the Lord (v. 6)?

EXPLORING WITH OTHERS

SUNDAY | Enjoying the View

Near the very end of the Bible, a passage describes the Lord Jesus as King of kings. How does Revelation 19:11–16 describe this King?

Sermon Title

Sermon Text

Sermon Notes

My Response

EXPEDITION 19: A FORK IN THE ROAD

OUR MAP

Explorers often have to choose between two paths. One goes to the right and one goes to the left, but which one do we take? That's the choice we find in the book of Proverbs. Its main author, King Solomon, describes two roads—Wise Road and Foolish Road—and calls us to choose Wise Road and run from Foolish Road. We should listen to King Solomon because he was one of the wisest people ever (1 Kings 4:29–34).

PRAYER POINTS

SNAPSHOT VERSE

Proverbs 1:7

DAILY LOG

MONDAY | Wisdom Teaches

 Proverbs 1:1–7

 Why did Solomon write Proverbs (v. 4)?

TUESDAY | Wisdom Appeals

 Proverbs 1:8–14

 Whose instruction should you listen to (v. 8)?

WEDNESDAY | Wisdom Warns

 Proverbs 1:15–19

 Why is it dangerous to walk in the foolish path of sinners (v. 15–16)?

THURSDAY | Wisdom Calls

 Proverbs 1:20–23

 What will Wisdom do if we repent and listen to it (v. 23)?

FRIDAY | Wisdom Threatens

 Proverbs 1:24–27

 What will Wisdom do if we do not listen to it (v. 26)?

SATURDAY | Wisdom Secures

 Proverbs 1:28–33

 Proverbs 1:33

EXPLORING WITH OTHERS

SUNDAY | Enjoying the View

What two images did Jesus use to present the choice between wisdom and folly (Matthew 7:13–14; 24–29)?

Sermon Title

Sermon Text

Sermon Notes

My Response

EXPEDITION 20: THE CHOICE

OUR MAP

Throughout Proverbs, King Solomon keeps reminding us of the choice between Wise Road and Foolish Road. Last week we looked at Solomon's longer descriptions of these two roads. This week we'll look at a number of snapshots that keep making us choose between Wise Road and Foolish Road.

PRAYER POINTS

SNAPSHOT VERSE

Proverbs 14:27

DAILY LOG

MONDAY | Foolish Lies

 Proverbs 14:1–5

 Who tells lies (v. 5)?

TUESDAY | Foolish Laughter

 Proverbs 14:6–11

 What do fools do to sin (the guilt offering) (v. 9)?

WEDNESDAY | Foolish Confidence

 Proverbs 14:12–16

 Proverbs 14:12

THURSDAY | Wise Love

 Proverbs 14:17–21

 What will make you happy (blessed) (v. 21)?

FRIDAY | Wise Fear

 Proverbs 14:22–29

 What will the fear of the Lord give you (vv. 26–27)?

SATURDAY | Wise Nation

 Proverbs 14:30–35

 What will make a nation great (v. 34)?

EXPLORING WITH OTHERS

SUNDAY | Enjoying the View

Solomon was the wisest man who had ever lived up to that point. But who was wiser than Solomon (1 Corinthians 1:24; Matthew 12:42; Colossians 2:3)?

Sermon Title

Sermon Text

Sermon Notes

My Response

EXPEDITION 21: A DANGEROUS DETOUR

OUR MAP

In addition to Proverbs, Solomon wrote two other books—Ecclesiastes and Song of Solomon. Ecclesiastes tells us of a time when Solomon, despite being so wise, chose the path of sinful folly and ended up desperately unhappy. It's a book to warn us against following him down this road.

PRAYER POINTS

SNAPSHOT VERSE

Ecclesiastes 12:1

DAILY LOG

MONDAY | Work without God

 Ecclesiastes 1:12–18

 How did Solomon describe everything under the sun (v. 14)?

TUESDAY | Pleasure without God

 Ecclesiastes 2:1–6

 What did Solomon try to make him happy (v. 1)?

WEDNESDAY | Possessions without God

 Ecclesiastes 2:7–11

 What phrase keeps appearing in this book (v. 11)?

THURSDAY | Education without God

 Ecclesiastes 2:12–17

 Ecclesiastes 2:17

FRIDAY | Wealth without God

 Ecclesiastes 2:18–23

 How did Solomon describe his life when he chose the wrong path (v. 23)?

SATURDAY | A Little with God

 Ecclesiastes 2:24–26; 12:13–14

 What did Solomon say after he had tried the wrong path (12:13)?

EXPLORING WITH OTHERS

SUNDAY | Enjoying the View

Solomon had everything, yet he had nothing. He had a great job, loads of money, a beautiful house, many friends, the best education, and many pleasures. But life without God just made him feel sad and empty. When he put God at the center of his life, even the simplest things like eating, drinking, and working gave him happiness and satisfaction (Ecclesiastes 2:24–25). Someone in the New Testament was very like Solomon (Matthew 19:16–22). What warning did Jesus give about him (Matthew 19:23–24)?

Sermon Title

Sermon Text

Sermon Notes

My Response

EXPEDITION 22: LOVE SONGS

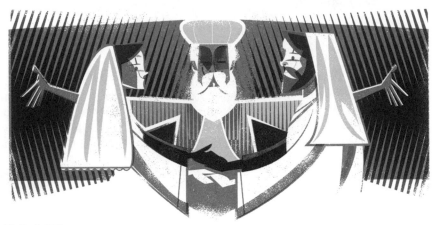

OUR MAP

I have many happy memories of family vacations when I was young. I can still remember the songs we used to sing in the car and where we were going when we sang them. Songs stick in our minds and help us to remember. Perhaps that's why God gave us the Song of Solomon or, as some Bibles entitle it, the "Song of Songs" (Song of Solomon 1:1). It's the best song ever because it describes the best love ever. It describes the love between a husband and a wife, but that man-woman love is also a picture or symbol of the love between God and Israel (Isaiah 54:5; Jeremiah 3:14) and between Christ and his church (Ephesians 5:23, 25).

PRAYER POINTS

SNAPSHOT VERSE

Song of Solomon 1:4

DAILY LOG

MONDAY | Love Is Passionate

 Song of Solomon 1:1–4

 What did the bride want the bridegroom to do (v. 2)?

TUESDAY | Love Is Public

 Song of Solomon 2:1–7

 What was on the banner over the shared feast (v. 4)?

WEDNESDAY | Love Is Lively

 Song of Solomon 2:8–13

 Song of Solomon 2:10

THURSDAY | Love Is Two-Way

 Song of Solomon 2:14–17

 Song of Solomon 2:16

FRIDAY | Love Is Longing

 Song of Solomon 3:1–5

 What did the bride do when she found the bridegroom again (v. 4)?

SATURDAY | Love Is Joyful

 Song of Solomon 3:6–11

 Describe Solomon's heart on his wedding day (v. 11).

EXPLORING WITH OTHERS

SUNDAY | Enjoying the View

As you look ahead to the rest of your life, you can pray that God would give you such a happy marriage as the one in the Song of Solomon. But even more, you can pray to be married to the Lord. Do you love him with a passionate, public, lively, two-way, seeking, and joyful love?

Sermon Title

Sermon Text

Sermon Notes

My Response

EXPEDITION 23: LOOKING INTO THE DISTANCE

OUR MAP

We're coming to the end of our exploration of the Old Testament. We've seen that God promised a special King who would deliver his people and defeat their enemies. Thus far we've been disappointed. But we mustn't give up hope of arriving at that destination. The prophets didn't. These were men whom God raised up and sent to his people to call them from their sins and to keep them hoping and looking for a great King and a great kingdom. Let's explore the Prophets together and discover some of their wonderful promises.

PRAYER POINTS

SNAPSHOT VERSE

Isaiah 9:6

DAILY LOG

MONDAY | A Godly King

 Isaiah 7:10–16

 What does *Immanuel* mean (Matthew 1:23)?

TUESDAY | A Worldwide King

 Isaiah 9:2–7

 What are the names of this special child (v. 6)?

WEDNESDAY | A Wise King

 Isaiah 11:1–5

 What kind of spirit will be in this special King (v. 2)?

THURSDAY | A Gentle King

 Isaiah 42:1–7

 Isaiah 42:3

FRIDAY | A Suffering King

 Isaiah 53:1–6

 What will people do to this special King (v. 3)?

SATURDAY | A Victorious King

 Isaiah 53:7–12

 Which verses speak of the King's victory?

EXPLORING WITH OTHERS

SUNDAY | Enjoying the View

Look at the way the prophets' predictions were fulfilled in Jesus many hundreds of years later:

Isaiah 7:14 and Matthew 1:23
Isaiah 9:6 and Luke 2:11–12
Isaiah 11:1 and Revelation 22:16

Isaiah 42:3 and Matthew 12:20
Isaiah 53:5–6 and 1 Peter 2:22–24
Isaiah 53:9 and Matthew 27:57–60

What does this tell us about the Bible?

Sermon Title

Sermon Text

Sermon Notes

My Response

EXPEDITION 24: THE GROWING EXCITEMENT

OUR MAP

As we finish our travels through the Old Testament, we learn even more about God's promised King. In addition to Isaiah, we hear from Jeremiah, Jonah, and Zechariah. They all increase our excitement and leave us on the edge of our seats, longing to see this long-awaited King. Who is he, and when will he come?

PRAYER POINTS

SNAPSHOT VERSE | Isaiah 61:1

DAILY LOG

MONDAY | The King Gives Light

 Isaiah 60:1–5

 How will the Gentiles (or nations) respond to this King (v. 3)?

TUESDAY | The King Releases Prisoners

 Isaiah 61:1–6

 What will this King preach (v. 1)?

WEDNESDAY | The King Forgives Sin

 Jeremiah 31:31–34

 What will God do for sinners (v. 34)?

Bridge: We remember the prophet Jonah because he was swallowed by a big fish. You can read about that in Jonah 1–2. But Jonah was also a powerful preacher. God the King used him to warn sinners and give repentance.

THURSDAY | The King Warns Sinners

 Jonah 3:1–4

 What was Jonah's message (v. 4)?

FRIDAY | The King Gives Repentance

 Jonah 3:5–10

 What did God do when the Ninevites repented (v. 10)?

SATURDAY | The King Provides Cleansing

 Zechariah 12:9–13:1

 What (or who) is the fountain opened for sin (13:1; 1 John 2:1–2)?

EXPLORING WITH OTHERS

SUNDAY | Enjoying the View

The prophets' predictions were fulfilled in Jesus. Match the prophecies with the fulfillment.

Isaiah 60:6
Isaiah 61:1–2
Jeremiah 31:34
Jonah 3
Zechariah 12:10

Matthew 2:11
Luke 4:18–19
Hebrews 8:12
Matthew 12:41
Acts 2:36–37

Sermon Title

Sermon Text

Sermon Notes

My Response

EXPEDITION 25: A STRANGE PALACE

OUR MAP

We've traveled many miles and many years in our journey through the Old Testament. We've explored many thick forests of biblical history. But we've also enjoyed many bright and beautiful views of a coming King. Now, after such a long wait, we're about to meet the King. God has given us four books about his life—the Gospels of Matthew, Mark, Luke, and John. Try to think of these four books as four different cameras that look at Jesus's life from four different angles. Over the next weeks we will be viewing the most important points in Jesus's life using each of these four cameras. We start with the birth of this King and the unusual palace he was born in.

PRAYER POINTS

SNAPSHOT VERSE | Matthew 1:21

DAILY LOG

MONDAY | The Baby's Parents

 Matthew 1:1–2 and 15–17

 Jesus is described as the son of
_____ (v. 1).

TUESDAY | The Baby's First Name

 Matthew 1:18–21

 Why was Mary's child called
Jesus (v. 21)?

WEDNESDAY | The Baby's Second Name

 Matthew 1:22–25

 What did Joseph call his son
(v. 25)?

THURSDAY | The Baby's Crib

 Luke 2:1–7

 Where was Jesus born (Luke 2:7)?

FRIDAY | The Baby's Choir

 Luke 2:8–14

 What did the angels sing (v. 14)?

SATURDAY | The Baby's Impact

 Luke 2:15–20

 How did the shepherds react to the baby (v. 20)?

EXPLORING WITH OTHERS

SUNDAY | Living in the Kingdom

The angels sang that this King would be a source of great joy to all people (Luke 2:10). What makes you joyful when you think about this King?

Sermon Title

Sermon Text

Sermon Notes

My Response

EXPEDITION 26: A TEMPLE AND A RIVER

OUR MAP

The Bible describes one important event in Jesus's childhood—the time he visited the temple when he was twelve years old. The next time we see Jesus, he is about thirty years old and is being baptized by John the Baptist in the river Jordan just before beginning his public ministry. Let's look at both of these events.

 PRAYER POINTS

 SNAPSHOT VERSE | Luke 2:52

DAILY LOG

MONDAY | Jesus Grows Up

 Luke 2:39–42

 Luke 2:40

TUESDAY | Jesus Teaches the Teachers

 Luke 2:43–47

 How did the people in the temple react to Jesus (v. 47)?

WEDNESDAY | Jesus Submits to His Parents

 Luke 2:48–52

 How did Jesus respond to his parents (v. 51)?

THURSDAY | John the Baptist Announces Jesus

 Mark 1:1–8

 What did John the Baptist preach (v. 4)?

FRIDAY | John Baptizes Jesus in the Jordan

 Mark 1:9–13

 What did the voice from heaven say to Jesus (v. 11)?

SATURDAY | Jesus Calls to Repentance

 Mark 1:14–18

 What was Jesus's first message (v. 15)?

EXPLORING WITH OTHERS

SUNDAY | Living in the Kingdom

Jesus announced the setting up of his kingdom and called people to enter it. How do we get into the kingdom (Mark 1:15)?

Sermon Title

Sermon Text

Sermon Notes

My Response

EXPEDITION 27: A CHURCH ON A MOUNTAIN

OUR MAP

Jesus's most famous sermon is his Sermon on the Mount. Let's stop on that hillside for a while and listen to his wonderful preaching. We begin with the Beatitudes, which describe the blessed character of the citizens in Christ's kingdom. After that we will look at the conduct of these citizens, how they are to live in this world.

PRAYER POINTS

SNAPSHOT VERSE

Matthew 5:3

DAILY LOG

MONDAY | Kingdom Character (1)

 Matthew 5:1–6

 What is given to the poor in spirit (v. 3)?

TUESDAY | Kingdom Character (2)

 Matthew 5:7–12

 Who will see God (v. 8)?

WEDNESDAY | Kingdom Light

 Matthew 5:13–16

 What are Christians to do in the world (v. 16)?

THURSDAY | Kingdom Fulfillment

 Matthew 5:17–20

 What did Jesus come to do with the Law and the Prophets (v. 17)?

FRIDAY | Kingdom Judgment

 Matthew 5:21–26

 What puts us in danger of God's judgment (v. 22)?

SATURDAY | Kingdom Marriage

 Matthew 5:27–32

 Matthew 27:30

EXPLORING WITH OTHERS

SUNDAY | Living in the Kingdom

We read about the character of the citizens in God's kingdom in Matthew 5:1–12. Which of these marks do you see in your own life?

Sermon Title

Sermon Text

Sermon Notes

My Response

EXPEDITION 28: ENEMIES

OUR MAP

Sometimes, explorers can encounter enemies in their travels. But in this part of Jesus's sermon, we'll discover that Jesus has a very unusual way of dealing with enemies.

PRAYER POINTS

SNAPSHOT VERSE

Matthew 5:48

DAILY LOG

MONDAY | Kingdom Words

 Matthew 5:33–37

 Matthew 5:37

TUESDAY | Kingdom Kindness

 Matthew 5:38–42

 Matthew 5:42

WEDNESDAY | Kingdom Enemies

 Matthew 5:43–48

 What should we do to our personal enemies (v. 44)?

THURSDAY | Kingdom Giving

 Matthew 6:1–4

 What will God do if we secretly give money to the church or to someone in need (v. 4)?

FRIDAY | Kingdom Religion

 Mathew 6:5–8

 What does God know before we pray (v. 8)?

SATURDAY | Kingdom Prayer

 Matthew 6:9–15

 What will happen if we do not forgive others (v. 15)?

EXPLORING WITH OTHERS

Prayer is so important in kingdom life. What was the most important lesson you learned about prayer from the model prayer that Jesus gave us in Matthew 6:9–13?

Sermon Title

Sermon Text

Sermon Notes

My Response

EXPEDITION 29: HEAVENLY TREASURE

OUR MAP

This is a long sermon isn't it? But because *Jesus* was preaching the Sermon on the Mount, I'm sure it wasn't boring. In this part he teaches us about money and worry. He also tells us what we should seek first in our travels.

PRAYER POINTS

SNAPSHOT VERSE | Matthew 6:33

DAILY LOG

MONDAY | Kingdom Fasting

 Matthew 6:16–18

 Where is fasting to take place (v. 18)?

TUESDAY | Kingdom Treasure

 Matthew 6:19–21

 Matthew 6:21

WEDNESDAY | Kingdom Light

 Matthew 6:22–24

 What is impossible to do (v. 24)?

THURSDAY | Kingdom Peace

 Matthew 6:25–30

 Where does Jesus point us to help us stop worrying (v. 26)?

FRIDAY | Kingdom First

 Matthew 6:31–34

 What are we to seek first (v. 33)?

SATURDAY | Kingdom Judgment

 Mathew 7:1–6

 What should we do first (v. 5)?

EXPLORING WITH OTHERS

SUNDAY | Living in the Kingdom

What does it mean to seek the kingdom of God first (Matthew 6:33)? How do we do that? If the kingdom of God should be first in our lives, what kinds of things should be in second, third, and fourth place?

Sermon Title

Sermon Text

Sermon Notes

My Response

EXPEDITION 30: TWO HOUSES

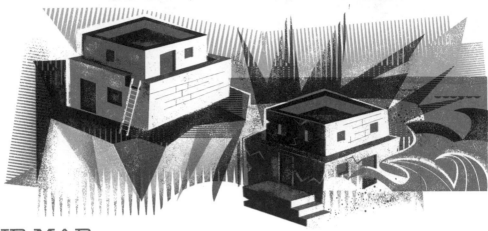

OUR MAP

One of the reasons the Sermon on the Mount is so interesting and enjoyable is that Jesus uses so many pictures, images, and stories to illustrate his teaching. As he finishes his sermon, he uses the pictures of door-knocking, road travel, fruit trees, and house-building. He uses these pictures to call us to enter his kingdom and live a kingdom life.

 PRAYER POINTS

 SNAPSHOT VERSE | Two verses this week, but they are similar in many ways: Matthew 7:24, 26.

DAILY LOG

MONDAY | Knocking on the Kingdom's Door

 Matthew 7:7-12

 Matthew 7:8

TUESDAY | Traveling the Kingdom's Road

 Matthew 7:13-14

 Describe the narrow way (v. 14).

WEDNESDAY | Bearing Kingdom Fruit

 Matthew 7:15-20

 How do we know if a tree is good or bad (v. 20)?

THURSDAY | Doing the Kingdom's Will

 Matthew 7:21–23

 Who will enter the kingdom of heaven (v. 21)?

FRIDAY | Building on Kingdom Rock

 Matthew 7:24–27

 Describe what happened to the two houses in the storm (vv. 25, 27).

SATURDAY | Responding to Kingdom Teaching

 Matthew 7:28–29

 How did people respond to Jesus's sermon (v. 28)?

EXPLORING WITH OTHERS

SUNDAY | Living in the Kingdom

The end of Jesus's Sermon on the Mount challenges us to ask, "Am I building on rock or sand?" What is it to build on the rock and what is it to build on the sand? What are you building on and how do you know?

Sermon Title

Sermon Text

Sermon Notes

My Response

EXPEDITION 31: A SAD WEDDING AND A DIRTY TEMPLE

OUR MAP

We've just heard Jesus's first sermon. Now let's see Jesus's first miracle, followed by his cleansing of the temple. Then we'll skip ahead to the book of 1 Peter to see what he teaches about the temple.

 PRAYER POINTS

 SNAPSHOT VERSE | John 2:16

DAILY LOG

MONDAY | A Sad Wedding

 John 2:1–5

 What did Jesus's mother say to the servants (v. 5)?

TUESDAY | A Happy Wedding

 John 2:6–11

 What did the disciples do when they saw the miracle (v. 11)?

WEDNESDAY | A Dirty Temple

 John 2:13–17

 Why was Jesus angry (v. 16)?

THURSDAY | A New Temple

 John 2:18–22

 What temple was Jesus speaking about (vv. 21–22)?

FRIDAY | A Living Temple

 1 Peter 2:1–6

 Who are the stones in Jesus's new temple (v. 4–5)?

SATURDAY | A Preaching Temple

 1 Peter 2:7–10

 What does this new temple do (v. 9)?

EXPLORING WITH OTHERS

SUNDAY | Living in the Kingdom

The Bible sometimes uses wine as a symbol of joy (Judges 9:13; Psalm 104:14–15)? How does Jesus bring joy to your life?

Sermon Title

Sermon Text

Sermon Notes

My Response

EXPEDITION 32: A NIGHTTIME VISITOR

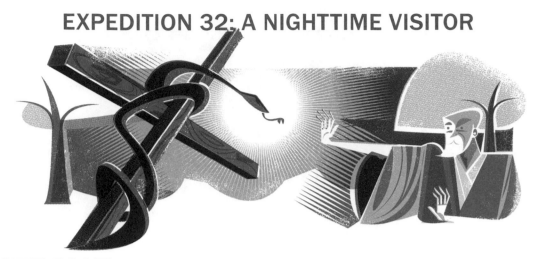

OUR MAP

We learn so much about Jesus from his sermons and his miracles. But we also learn a lot from listening to his conversations with others who needed to hear the gospel. This week we listen in on a conversation between Jesus and Nicodemus, an important religious leader. He visited Jesus in the middle of the night because he was afraid to be seen talking to Jesus.

PRAYER POINTS

SNAPSHOT VERSE | John 3:16

DAILY LOG

MONDAY | A New Birth

 John 3:1–4

 John 3:3

TUESDAY | A Powerful Wind

 John 3:5–10

 What must happen (v. 7)?

WEDNESDAY | A Saving Snake

 John 3:11–15

 What did Moses lift up in the wilderness (v. 14)?

THURSDAY | A Sending Love

 John 3:16–21

 Why did God send his Son into the world (v. 17)?

FRIDAY | A Beautiful Humility

 John 3:25–30

 John 3:30

SATURDAY | A Clear Choice

 John 3:31–36

 John 3:36

EXPLORING WITH OTHERS

SUNDAY | Living in the Kingdom

In what way was Moses's lifting up of the serpent like Jesus being lifted up? (Read Numbers 21:4–9 and John 3:14.)

Sermon Title

Sermon Text

Sermon Notes

My Response

EXPEDITION 33: WATER IN THE DESERT

OUR MAP

In our last expedition we listened to Jesus talking to Nicodemus, a very religious man. In this expedition, we're going to travel to a well in a desert to listen to his conversation with a Samaritan woman, a very sinful woman.

PRAYER POINTS

SNAPSHOT VERSE | John 4:14

DAILY LOG

MONDAY | Jesus Asks for a Drink

 John 4:5–8

 Why did Jesus sit by the well (v. 6)?

TUESDAY | Jesus Offers a Drink

 John 4:9–14

 What will happen to those who drink of Jesus's water (v. 14)?

WEDNESDAY | Jesus Creates Thirst

 John 4:15–21

 How many husbands did the woman have (v. 18)?

THURSDAY | Jesus Wants Worshipers

 John 4:22-27

 John 4:24

FRIDAY | Jesus Saves a Sinner

 John 4:28-34

 What did the woman say (v. 29)?

SATURDAY | Jesus Saves Many Sinners

 John 4:39-42

 How did the Samaritans describe Jesus (v. 42)?

EXPLORING WITH OTHERS

SUNDAY | Living in the Kingdom

Jesus came to save sinners from all over the world (John 4:42). What can you do to get the message of Jesus to the whole world?

Sermon Title

Sermon Text

Sermon Notes

My Response

EXPEDITION 34: WONDERS OF THE WORLD

OUR MAP

Just as ancient explorers discovered the seven Wonders of the World, this week's expedition will discover some of Jesus's wonders. We will see people wowed by his wonderful healings, and then the disciples wowed by his wonderful glory.

PRAYER POINTS

SNAPSHOT VERSE | Mark 2:5

DAILY LOG

MONDAY | Jesus Amazes with His Power

 Mark 1:23–28

 Who did the unclean spirit know Jesus was (v. 24)?

TUESDAY | Jesus Heals Multitudes

 Mark 1:29–35

 What did Jesus do first thing in the morning (v. 35)?

WEDNESDAY | Jesus Cleanses a Leper

 Mark 1:40–45

 What did Jesus say to the leper (v. 41)?

THURSDAY | Jesus Forgives the Guilty

 Mark 2:1–5

 What did Jesus say to the lame man (v. 5)?

FRIDAY | Jesus Enables the Disabled

 Mark 2:6–12

 What does Jesus have power to do (v. 10)?

SATURDAY | Jesus Shines Like the Sun

 Mark 9:2–8

 What did Jesus look like on the mountain (v. 3)?

EXPLORING WITH OTHERS

SUNDAY | Living in the Kingdom

We've seen some amazing wonders this past week. Jesus has healed many people of many diseases and problems. What's the greatest healing Jesus can offer (Mark 2:5, 10)? Have you been healed in this way?

Sermon Title

Sermon Text

Sermon Notes

My Response

EXPEDITION 35: LOST AND FOUND

OUR MAP

If we were to follow the Bible perfectly, we would never go astray and get lost. But when we disobey or forget the Bible and end up lost, what then? Is there any hope for us? Can we ever get back on track? To find out, we're going to explore three of Jesus's parables. Parables are earthly stories with heavenly meanings. The three parables in this week's expedition will take us to a mountainside, a house, and a pigpen in a faraway country.

 PRAYER POINTS

 SNAPSHOT VERSE | Luke 15:10

DAILY LOG

MONDAY | The Lost Sheep

 Luke 15:1–7

 What does the shepherd do when one of his sheep gets lost (v. 4)?

TUESDAY | The Lost Coin

 Luke 15:8–10

 What did the lady say to her neighbors when she found the lost coin (v. 9)?

WEDNESDAY | The Lost Son

 Luke 15:11–16

 What did the Prodigal Son do in the faraway country (v. 13)?

THURSDAY | A Father Finds His Son

 Luke 15:17–21

 What did the Prodigal say to his Father (v. 21)?

FRIDAY | A Father Rejoices Over His Son

 Luke 15:22–27

 What did the father order to be put on his son (v. 22)?

SATURDAY | A Father Rebukes His Son

 Luke 15:28–32

 Why was the father so happy (v. 32)?

EXPLORING WITH OTHERS

SUNDAY | Living in the Kingdom

What do these three parables tell us about God?
What do they tell us about how we should view those who go astray and get lost?

Sermon Title

Sermon Text

Sermon Notes

My Response

EXPEDITION 36: A SHEPHERD, A SERVANT, A VINEDRESSER, AND A BUILDER

OUR MAP

Jesus loved to teach using pictures. This week we'll explore four pictures he used to describe himself: a shepherd to guide us, a servant to care for us, a builder to prepare a home for us, and a vine that makes us fruitful.

 PRAYER POINTS

 SNAPSHOT VERSE | John 14:6

DAILY LOG

MONDAY | The Shepherd Calls His Sheep

 John 10:1-6

 Why do sheep follow their shepherd (v. 4)?

TUESDAY | The Shepherd Saves His Sheep

 John 10:7-13

 John 10:11

WEDNESDAY | The Shepherd Protects His Sheep

 John 10:14-18

 What does Jesus lay down for his sheep (v. 15)?

THURSDAY | The Servant Washes Feet

 John 13:1–7

 What did Jesus do when he knew that he was about to die (vv. 1, 5)?

FRIDAY | The Builder Prepares a Home

 John 14:1–6

 What is the father's house like and what is Jesus doing there (v. 2)?

SATURDAY | The Vine Produces Grapes

 John 15:1–8

 What must we do to produce good fruit in our lives (v. 4)?

EXPLORING WITH OTHERS

SUNDAY | Living in the Kingdom

In what way are you following the Shepherd's voice (John 10:4)?
In what way are you serving others (John 13:14)?
In what way are you bearing fruit (John 15:8)?

Sermon Title

Sermon Text

Sermon Notes

My Response

EXPEDITION 37: THE DARKEST NIGHT

OUR MAP

We're about to embark on the darkest part of our journey. We're going to walk alongside Jesus as he walks a path of suffering and death. After many years of teaching and healing, Jesus will be condemned to death. The light of the world will be put out by the darkness of the world. But don't fear: there is a happy ending to this saddest of stories.

PRAYER POINTS

SNAPSHOT VERSE

Matthew 26:28

DAILY LOG

MONDAY | Jesus Covenants

 Matthew 26:26–30

 What do the bread and wine picture (vv. 26–28)?

TUESDAY | Jesus Warns

 Matthew 26:31–35

 What did Jesus say the disciples would do (v. 31)?

WEDNESDAY | Jesus Prays

 Matthew 26:36–41

 Matthew 26:41

THURSDAY | Jesus Prepares

 Matthew 26:42–46

 What did Jesus pray (v. 42)?

FRIDAY | Jesus Is Betrayed

 Matthew 26:47–50

 What did Judas do and say to Jesus (v. 49)?

SATURDAY | Jesus Is Abandoned

 Matthew 26:51–56

 What did the disciples do (v. 56)?

EXPLORING WITH OTHERS

SUNDAY | Living in the Kingdom

Can you think of ways you might be tempted to run away from Jesus like the disciples did? What should you do instead?

Sermon Title

Sermon Text

Sermon Notes

My Response

EXPEDITION 38: THE DARKEST TRIAL

OUR MAP

Jesus was tried in a Jewish court, a royal court, and a Roman court. All three courts were unfair and unjust in condemning Jesus without any good reason.

 PRAYER POINTS

 SNAPSHOT VERSE | 1 Peter 2:23

DAILY LOG

MONDAY | Jesus Accused

 Matthew 26:57–61

 Describe the witnesses against Jesus (vv. 59–60).

TUESDAY | Jesus Sentenced

 Matthew 26:62–68

 What was the court's sentence against Jesus (v. 66)?

WEDNESDAY | Jesus Denied

 Matthew 26:69–75

 What did Peter do when he realized his sin (v. 75)?

THURSDAY | Jesus Delivered

 Matthew 27:1-5

 What did the chief priests and elders plot to do (v. 1)?

FRIDAY | Jesus Is Silent

 Matthew 27:12-18

 How did Jesus respond to the accusations (v. 14)?

SATURDAY | Jesus Exchanged

 Matthew 27:19-26

 Whom did the people ask to be released instead of Jesus (vv. 20, 26)?

EXPLORING WITH OTHERS

SUNDAY | Living in the Kingdom

Peter sinned very seriously by denying three times that he knew Jesus. Yet after Jesus rose from the dead, Jesus drew Peter back to him. How did he do that (Mark 16:7; John 21:15–17)?

Sermon Title

Sermon Text

Sermon Notes

My Response

EXPEDITION 39: THE DARKEST DEATH

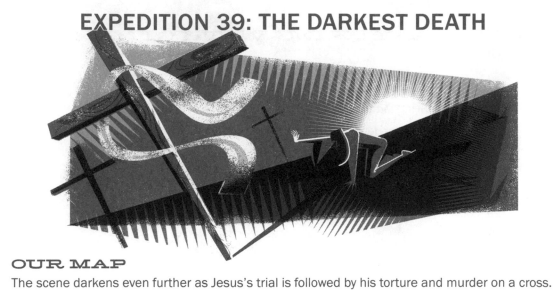

OUR MAP

The scene darkens even further as Jesus's trial is followed by his torture and murder on a cross.

 PRAYER POINTS

 SNAPSHOT VERSE | Luke 23:42

DAILY LOG

MONDAY | Jesus Stripped

 Matthew 27:27–33

 What did the soldiers put on Jesus's head (v. 29)?

TUESDAY | Jesus Crucified

 Matthew 27:34–38

 What did the soldiers write above the cross (v. 37)?

WEDNESDAY | Jesus Mocked

 Matthew 27:39–44

 What did the robbers do (v. 44)?

THURSDAY | Jesus Saves

 Luke 23:39–43

 What did Jesus say to the repentant thief (v. 43)?

FRIDAY | Jesus Forsaken

 Matthew 27:45–49

 What did Jesus say to God (v. 46)?

SATURDAY | Jesus Dies

 Matthew 27:50–56

 What did the centurion say when Jesus died (v. 54)?

EXPLORING WITH OTHERS

SUNDAY | Living in the Kingdom

What is the meaning of Jesus's death for you (1 Peter 2:24)?

Sermon Title

Sermon Text

Sermon Notes

My Response

EXPEDITION 40: THE BRIGHTEST MORNING

OUR MAP

The King is dead. Long live the King! Although the past expedition was shrouded in darkness as Jesus was crucified, in this expedition we'll see the sun rise again and shine more brightly than ever.

PRAYER POINTS

SNAPSHOT VERSE

| Matthew 28:19

DAILY LOG

MONDAY | A Dead Body

 Matthew 27:57–61

 What did Joseph do with Jesus's body (v. 60)?

TUESDAY | A Sealed Tomb

 Matthew 27:62–66

 What did the Pharisees do to the tomb (v. 66)?

WEDNESDAY | An Open Tomb

 Matthew 28:1–4

 Matthew 28:2

THURSDAY | An Empty Tomb

 Matthew 28:5-8

 Matthew 28:6

FRIDAY | A Great Celebration

 Matthew 28:9-15

 What did the women do when they saw Jesus (v. 9)?

SATURDAY | A Great Commission

 Matthew 28:16-20

 What promise did Jesus give to his disciples (v. 20)?

EXPLORING WITH OTHERS

SUNDAY | Living in the Kingdom

In Matthew 28:19–20 Jesus calls his followers to go and tell all nations about the gospel. How will you do that in your daily life?

Sermon Title

Sermon Text

Sermon Notes

My Response

EXPEDITION 41: THE GOSPEL FOR THE WORLD

OUR MAP

Up until now, our expeditions have been mainly centered on Israel, a small country in the Middle East. Now, the apostles are about to take the gospel into all the world as Jesus commanded them. The book of Acts begins with Jesus ascending to heaven and giving his disciples two promises. The first is that they would receive the Holy Spirit to make them witnesses to Christ (Acts 1:8). The second was that he would return again to earth in the same way he had left it (Acts 1:11). This brings us to the day of Pentecost, when the first of these promises would be fulfilled in a wonderful way.

PRAYER POINTS

SNAPSHOT VERSE

Acts 2:21

17/3

DAILY LOG

MONDAY | Full of the Spirit

 Acts 2:1–6

 What were the disciples filled with (v. 4)?

 holy spirit

TUESDAY | Full of Wine?

 Acts 2:7–13

 What amazed the people (vv. 7–8)?

WEDNESDAY | Full of Courage

 Acts 2:14–21

 Which prophet's prediction came true at Pentecost (v. 16)?

THURSDAY | Full of Good News

 Acts 2:22–24, 36–39

 Acts 2:39

FRIDAY | Full of Believers

 Acts 2:40–43

 How many people were converted to Christ that day (v. 41)?

SATURDAY | Full of Love

 Acts 2:44–47

 What did people do with their possessions (vv. 44–45)?

EXPLORING WITH OTHERS

SUNDAY | Living in the Kingdom

After Jesus's Sermon on the Mount, Peter's sermon at Pentecost is probably the most famous sermon in the world. It was full of truth, full of the Spirit, and full of power, and it resulted in a full church. What kinds of activities were in the first New Testament church in Acts 2:46–47?

Sermon Title

Sermon Text

Sermon Notes

My Response

EXPEDITION 42: THE MOST FAMOUS ROAD IN THE WORLD

OUR MAP

Have you ever heard of the Damascus Road? The most famous conversion happened there. Let's travel along it and see what God did to change Saul of Tarsus into the apostle Paul.

 PRAYER POINTS

 SNAPSHOT VERSE | Acts 9:15

DAILY LOG

MONDAY | Persecuting Saul

 Acts 9:1–5

 What was Saul's first question (v. 5)?

TUESDAY | Blind Saul

 Acts 9:6–9

 Describe Saul's condition (v. 9).

WEDNESDAY | Chosen Saul

 Acts 9:10–16

 Why was Ananias scared of Saul (vv. 13–14)?

THURSDAY | Preaching Saul

 Acts 9:17–20

 What did Saul immediately do (v. 20)?

FRIDAY | Growing Saul

 Acts 9:21–25

 Acts 9:22

SATURDAY | Courageous Saul

 Acts 9:26–31

 Describe the church in verse 31.

EXPLORING WITH OTHERS

SUNDAY | Living in the Kingdom

The first two signs that Saul of Tarsus was being converted to Christ were his asking about who Jesus was (Acts 9:5) and about what Jesus wanted him to do (v. 6). Do you see these two marks in your own life? In what ways do you try to find out more about Jesus and obey his will rather than your own?

Sermon Title

Sermon Text

Sermon Notes

My Response

EXPEDITION 43: THREE CONVERSIONS

OUR MAP

After his conversion, the apostle Paul traveled everywhere preaching Christ. As a result, Saul the persecutor became Paul the persecuted. In Acts 16, he ends up in the Philippi jail. But he also sees three people converted to Christ: a businesswoman, a slave girl, and a jailer. Three very different people. Three very different conversions.

PRAYER POINTS

SNAPSHOT VERSE

Acts 16:31

DAILY LOG

MONDAY | Salvation by the River

 Acts 16:9–15

 How was Lydia saved (v. 14)?

TUESDAY | Salvation on the Street

 Acts 16:16–19

 What did the slave girl cry out (v. 17)?

WEDNESDAY | Sentenced to Jail

 Acts 16:20–24

 How were Paul and Silas punished (vv. 22–23)?

THURSDAY | Singing in Jail

 Acts 16:25–28

 What did Paul and Silas do in the jail (v. 25)?

FRIDAY | Salvation in Jail

 Acts 16:29–34

 Why was the jailer so happy (v. 34)?

SATURDAY | Encouraged in Lydia's House

 Acts 16:35–40

 What did Paul and Silas do when they were released (v. 40)?

EXPLORING WITH OTHERS

SUNDAY | Living in the Kingdom

We've seen three beautiful conversions in the past week. They were all different though. For example, the Lord simply opened Lydia's heart to hear his Word (Acts 16:14). The jailer's conversion was sudden and dramatic, and it too resulted in him listening to God's Word. Why not ask a Christian you know how he or she came to faith in Christ?

Sermon Title

Sermon Text

Sermon Notes

My Response

EXPEDITION 44: ATHENS

OUR MAP

Having traveled hundreds of miles preaching the gospel and starting churches, Paul finds himself in Athens (Acts 17). As he walks around, he gets sad and angry about all the idols and all the people worshiping them. You won't be surprised to find out that he's soon preaching the gospel to them.

 PRAYER POINTS

 SNAPSHOT VERSE | Acts 17:30

DAILY LOG

MONDAY | Some Were Persuaded

 Acts 17:1–4

 What did Paul usually do when he came to a city (vv. 2–3)?

TUESDAY | Some Were Angry

 Acts 17:5–8

 What did the Jews of Thessalonica accuse the apostles of doing (v. 6)?

WEDNESDAY | Some Were Students

 Acts 17:10–15

 Acts 17:11

THURSDAY | Some Were Curious

 Acts 17:16–21

 How did Paul react to all the idols (v. 16)?

FRIDAY | Some Were Religious

 Acts 17:22–28

 Acts 17:27

SATURDAY | Some Were Mockers

 Acts 17:29–34

 Acts 17:31

EXPLORING WITH OTHERS

SUNDAY | Living in the Kingdom

We've seen many different responses to the gospel in Acts 17. What is your response to the gospel?

Sermon Title

Sermon Text

Sermon Notes

My Response

EXPEDITION 45: PREACHING TO THE KING

OUR MAP

After three eventful missionary journeys, the apostle Paul decided to go to Jerusalem and Rome to preach (Acts 19:21). Although his friends warned him against this, he said that he was even ready to die in Jerusalem for the name of the Lord Jesus (Acts 21:1–13). As expected, he was arrested there and sent to prison. After being tried in front of various judges (Acts 22–25), he was summoned to appear before King Agrippa in Caesarea (Acts 26). Let's listen in on Paul's thrilling defense before the king.

PRAYER POINTS

SNAPSHOT VERSE

Acts 26:18

DAILY LOG

MONDAY | I Was a Jew

 Acts 26:1–7

 Why was Paul being judged (vv. 6–7)?

TUESDAY | I Was a Persecutor

 Acts 26:8–11

 Acts 26:8

WEDNESDAY | I Am a Christian

 Acts 26:12–18

 Why was Paul sent to the Gentiles (v. 18)?

THURSDAY | I Am a Preacher

 Acts 26:19–23

 What was Paul's message (vv. 22–23)?

FRIDAY | I Am Not Crazy

 Acts 26:24–29

 How did King Agrippa respond to Paul's preaching (v. 28)?

SATURDAY | I Am a Prisoner

 Acts 26:30–32; 28:16; 28:30–31

 What did Paul do in Rome when he was kept as a prisoner in a house (v. 31)?

EXPLORING WITH OTHERS

SUNDAY | Living in the Kingdom

King Agrippa sent Paul to Rome to stand trial there. There was a lot of drama on the way! First, God delivered him from a storm and a shipwreck (Acts 27), and then God delivered him from a poisonous snakebite (Acts 28). But God did not deliver him from being a prisoner in Rome and standing trial there. That's because God had a higher and greater purpose for Paul than his freedom. Last week we saw the apostle using his time of imprisonment for advancing God's kingdom. But he also used the time to write many letters to various churches. We'll read some of these over the next few weeks. Can you think of a time when things went badly for you but God turned it for good?

Sermon Title

Sermon Text

Sermon Notes

My Response

EXPEDITION 46: THE OLD FAITHFUL GEYSER

OUR MAP

The apostle Paul sent a letter to the Roman Christians years before he arrived in Rome as a prisoner. In his letter he wrote about how much he longed to see and fellowship with them. Little did he think that he would arrive in chains! This letter contains many beautiful sections, but we have time to look at only one part. It's like having only one day to explore Yellowstone National Park. It's a difficult choice, but I've decided to lead you through Romans 8. This chapter in Romans is like the Old Faithful geyser at Yellowstone. It's deep, high, and full of power, and you never tire of looking at it.

 PRAYER POINTS

 **SNAPSHOT VERSE** | Romans 8:28

DAILY LOG

MONDAY | Walking in the Spirit

 Romans 8:1–5

 What kind of people are not condemned by God (v. 1)?

"in Christe Jesus

TUESDAY | Led by the Spirit

 Romans 8:11–17

 What does the Holy Spirit tell us (vv. 15–16)?

WEDNESDAY | Groaning by the Spirit

 Romans 8:18–25

 Romans 8:18

THURSDAY | Helped by the Spirit

 Romans 8:26–30

 How does the Holy Spirit help us (v. 26)?

FRIDAY | No Accusation

 Romans 8:31–34

 Romans 8:31

SATURDAY | No Separation

 Romans 8:35–39

 What can separate us from the love of Christ (vv. 38–39)?

EXPLORING WITH OTHERS

SUNDAY | Living in the Kingdom

There are three persons in the Godhead: God the Father, God the Son, and God the Holy Spirit. We need the Holy Spirit to apply salvation to our souls. Read over Romans 8 and note how many things the Holy Spirit does for the believer.

Sermon Title

Sermon Text

Sermon Notes

My Response

EXPEDITION 47: THE WAY OF LOVE

OUR MAP

The church in Corinth was divided. People were fighting with one another and following different preachers instead of following God. In his first letter to the Corinthians, the apostle Paul reminded the Christians there to focus on Christ not preachers (chap. 1), and to love one another as Christ loved the church (chap. 13). He also defended the Bible's teaching about the resurrection, which some in Corinth were denying (chap. 15).

 PRAYER POINTS

 SNAPSHOT VERSE | 1 Corinthians 15:21

DAILY LOG

MONDAY | God's Wisdom

 1 Corinthians 1:18–25

 What did Paul preach (v. 23)?

TUESDAY | God's Choice

 1 Corinthians 1:26–30

 What kind of people does God choose to save (vv. 26–28)?

WEDNESDAY | God's Love

 1 Corinthians 13:1–7

 What does love not do (vv. 4–6)?

THURSDAY | God's Face

 1 Corinthians 13:8–13

 Which is the greatest: faith, hope, or love (v. 13)?

FRIDAY | God's Resurrection

 1 Corinthians 15:12–19

 1 Corinthians 15:14

SATURDAY | God's Victory

 1 Corinthians 15:20–26

 What is the last enemy that God will destroy (v. 26)?

EXPLORING WITH OTHERS

SUNDAY | Living in the Kingdom

First Corinthians 13 is one of the most famous chapters in the Bible and is often read in churches. However, it's much harder to live 1 Corinthians 13 than to read it. How can you show chapter 13 love to others in your family?

Sermon Title

Sermon Text

Sermon Notes

My Response

EXPEDITION 48: THREE APPETIZERS

OUR MAP

Paul wrote short letters to the churches in Galatia, Ephesus, and Philippi, each one packed full of precious truth. We don't have time to read them all in an expedition that lasts just a week, but I hope that the brief samples we'll taste will give you an appetite for more.

PRAYER POINTS

SNAPSHOT VERSE

Philippians 2:10–11

DAILY LOG

MONDAY | Rotten Fruit

 Galatians 5:14–21

 What will happen if we bear rotten fruit (v. 21)?

TUESDAY | Good Fruit

 Galatians 5:22–26

 List the good fruit that the Holy Spirit produces (vv. 22–23).

WEDNESDAY | Husband and Wife

 Ephesians 5:22–27

 Who is the model for a husband? Who is the model for a wife (vv. 24–25)?

THURSDAY | Christ and the Church

 Ephesians 5:28–33

 Ephesians 5:31

FRIDAY | Our Problem of Selfishness

 Philippians 2:1–4

 How should you view others (v. 3)?

SATURDAY | Christ's Solution of Humility

 Philippians 2:5–11

 How many knees will bow to Christ and how many tongues will confess him (vv. 10–11)?

EXPLORING WITH OTHERS

SUNDAY | Living in the Kingdom

In the previous week's expedition, we explored the apostle Paul's beautiful teaching about love in 1 Corinthians 13. He returned to this theme in the three samples we tasted this week. Galatians 5 connects love for our neighbor with bearing good spiritual fruit. Ephesians 5 teaches that the loving relationship between Christ and his people is the model for married love. Philippians 2 shows us Christ's unselfish love as the model for our love. How do your Mom or Dad show love toward you?

Sermon Title

Sermon Text

Sermon Notes

My Response

EXPEDITION 49: THE HALL OF FAITH

OUR MAP

Many expeditions ago, we met a number of Old Testament heroes. Well, they're back! The letter to the Hebrews shows us that the Old Testament heroes were also believers. They had faith in God's promised Savior just like we do. They looked forward to him; we look back to him. But we are all looking to Jesus. The letter to the Hebrews also shows us how the Old Testament prophecies were fulfilled perfectly in the New Testament story of Jesus. Jesus is God's final sacrifice, God's final priest, God's final tabernacle, and God's final covenant.

PRAYER POINTS

SNAPSHOT VERSE

Hebrews 11:6

DAILY LOG

MONDAY | Faith Pleases God

 Hebrews 11:1–6

 If we do not have faith, what is impossible (v. 6)?

TUESDAY | Faith Looks for a City

 Hebrews 11:7–12

 What was Abraham looking forward to (v. 10)?

WEDNESDAY | Faith Helps Us to Die

 Hebrews 11:13–16

 How did the Old Testament heroes die (v. 13)?

THURSDAY | Faith Believes in Life after Death

 Hebrews 11:17–22

 What was Abraham thinking when he was about to sacrifice his son, Isaac (v. 19)?

FRIDAY | Faith Chooses Christ

 Hebrews 11:23–28

 Hebrews 11:26

SATURDAY | Faith Conquers Kingdoms

 Hebrews 11:32–40

 What did the Old Testament heroes do through faith (v. 33)?

EXPLORING WITH OTHERS

SUNDAY | Living in the Kingdom

Who is your favorite Old Testament hero and why?

Sermon Title

Sermon Text

Sermon Notes

My Response

EXPEDITION 50: A BURNING TONGUE AND A BURNING WORLD

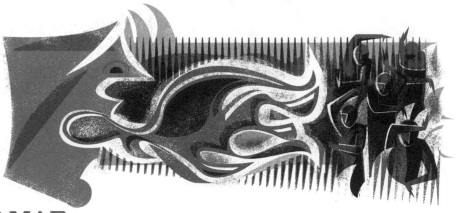

OUR MAP

Paul was not the only letter-writer. James, Peter, and John also wrote letters. They didn't write as many as Paul, and their letters were not as long as Paul's were. Let's look at some of the best-known chapters in their letters.

PRAYER POINTS

SNAPSHOT VERSE | 1 John 1:7

DAILY LOG

MONDAY | The Tongue Boasts

 James 3:1–5

 Describe the tongue (v. 5).

TUESDAY | The Tongue Burns

 James 3:6–12

 James 3:8

WEDNESDAY | The World Was Flooded

 2 Peter 3:1–7

 2 Peter 3:7

THURSDAY | The World Will Burn

 2 Peter 3:8-13

 What will happen to this earth when Jesus returns (v. 10)?

FRIDAY | The Cleansing of Sin

 1 John 1:1-7

 How does John describe God (v. 5)?

SATURDAY | The Confessing of Sin

 1 John 1:8-2:2

 What will happen if we confess our sins (1:9)?

EXPLORING WITH OTHERS

SUNDAY | Living in the Kingdom

James used a number of word-pictures to teach us how dangerous the tongue can be. List some of the images you find in James 3:3–8.

Sermon Title

Sermon Text

Sermon Notes

My Response

EXPEDITION 51: A REVELATION OF JESUS

OUR MAP

What a journey we've been on! We've covered many miles. We've seen many countries. We've met many people. We've read many words. But from beginning to end, all these miles, countries, people, and words have pointed to the Savior, Jesus Christ. Yes, we've been exploring the Bible. But we've also been exploring Jesus. We've discovered so much about him from our first expedition in Genesis until now.

So you won't be surprised that the last book of the Bible is also full of Jesus. In fact, its title is "The Revelation [or Unveiling] of Jesus Christ." It reveals Jesus to us, especially his love for his church in a hostile world.

 PRAYER POINTS

 SNAPSHOT VERSE | Revelation 1:7

DAILY LOG

MONDAY | Jesus the Faithful Witness

 Revelation 1:1–6

 How is Jesus Christ described (v. 5)?

TUESDAY | Jesus the Beginning and the End

 Revelation 1:7–11

 Revelation 1:8

WEDNESDAY | Jesus in the Middle of the Church

 Revelation 1:12–16

 Describe Jesus's eyes and voice (vv. 14–15).

THURSDAY | Jesus in His Glory

 Revelation 1:17–20

 What did John do when he saw Jesus (v. 17)?

FRIDAY | Jesus Speaks to the Loveless Church

 Revelation 2:1–7

 What had gone wrong in the church of Ephesus (v. 4)?

SATURDAY | Jesus Speaks to the Persecuted Church

 Revelation 2:8–11

 What will Jesus give to his faithful people (v. 10)?

EXPLORING WITH OTHERS

SUNDAY | Living in the Kingdom

The book of Revelation focuses on the end of the world and the return of Jesus Christ to judge everyone who has ever lived. How can you get ready for Christ's second coming?

Sermon Title

Sermon Text

Sermon Notes

My Response

EXPEDITION 52: THE NEW WORLD

OUR MAP

We started with an expedition to a beautiful garden (Genesis 1). We end with an expedition to a beautiful garden (Revelation 21–22). Although sin entered and damaged the first garden, God has prepared a new garden in the new heaven and the new earth for his people to enter and enjoy forever. In this last expedition through the last two chapters of the Bible, we see a glimpse of the beautiful new world that God has prepared for those who put their faith in Jesus Christ for everything.

PRAYER POINTS

SNAPSHOT VERSE

Revelation 22:20

DAILY LOG

MONDAY | The Comfort of Heaven

 Revelation 21:1–5

 Revelation 21:4

TUESDAY | The Light of Heaven

 Revelation 21:22–27

 Who will enter heaven (v. 27)?

WEDNESDAY | The Center of Heaven

 Revelation 22:1–5

 Why will there be no night in heaven (v. 5)?

THURSDAY | The Nearness of Heaven

 Revelation 22:6–11

 Who is blessed (v. 7)?

FRIDAY | The Holiness of Heaven

 Revelation 22:12–17

 How does Jesus describe himself (v. 16)?

SATURDAY | The Guide to Heaven

 Revelation 22:18–21

 What book is Jesus describing (vv. 18–19)?

EXPLORING WITH OTHERS

SUNDAY | Living in the Kingdom

Jesus is coming back to end the old world and begin the new world. From your reading in Revelation 21–22, what will the new heaven and earth be like?

Sermon Title

Sermon Text

Sermon Notes

My Response

THANKS FOR THE RIDE!

Well, my fellow-explorer, thank you for being my traveling companion over all these weeks. Believe it or not, we've just traveled the full length of the Bible together! We've gone from Genesis 1 to Revelation 22!

Now, of course, we didn't visit every chapter, but we explored some of the most important peaks in the Bible's story. I hope you agree that the view of God and of his salvation have been worth all the effort.

You should feel a bit less lost and confused now when you read the Bible. And that's what I encourage you to do—keep reading the Bible. The past year's joint exploration will help you to do some solo exploring.

Why not pick one of the Gospels and read it through in the same way as we did in this book? Pray for God's help, read a few verses a day, and ask yourself a question about what you've read or write out a verse.

Choose a verse to memorize every week. You might want to write these out on small cards so that you can keep them together in a box and review them from time to time.

When you've finished a Gospel, perhaps go to the Old Testament and work through Genesis, then go to the New Testament again, and so on.

And remember to keep exploring with others too—talk to your dad, your mom, and your pastor about what you are reading and ask them any questions you have. Keep up the good habit of taking some notes on your pastor's sermon and asking how you should respond to it.

The more you explore the Bible, the safer you will be as you grow up and move out into exploring the world.

God bless your future expeditions.

Your Fellow Explorer,
David Murray

NOTES

NOTES

NOTES

NOTES

NOTES